CHILDREN AND THEIR FATHERS

A  terra magica BOOK

HANNS REICH

Children and Their Fathers

TEXT BY EUGEN ROTH

HILL and WANG · NEW YORK
A division of Farrar, Straus and Giroux

"What's more, you're fresh!" Four–year–old Stephen, eyes flashing and lower lip thrust out, yells at his father. Yet papa was about to spank, not Stephen, but his eight–year–old brother. Stephen warns the old man not to butt in and tells him to go back to bed. A howl of laughter from "big" brother, an indulgent smile from mother, and the angry family quarrel comes to an end.

What fathers among us can't relate similar family incidents? Or perhaps some have long since decided that child–rearing is a science rather than an art. So they take the position that you should treat children "objectively"—and never lay a hand on them.

"You grown–ups take children much too seriously," asserts seven–year–old Thomas. This is his contribution, and an important one, to the age–old problem of bringing up children. As Democritus pointed out over two thousand years ago, it is at best an uncertain affair.

Anyhow, we fathers should only stop and think back a moment. What did our own fathers (not to mention our grandfathers) say, or rather do, when their offspring began to rebel at a tender age against their weighty authority?

Of course, living together for one or two decades, even in our rapidly changing world, develops a kind of pedagogical coexistence. But no one can deny that children have fundamentally changed. We read it every day in the newspapers or magazines; we hear it on the radio; and, if we go to the movies or sit in front of our television screens, we see it on film. But this in turn leads us to another conclusion. By and large we parents—especially we *fathers*—have changed. Let us console ourselves by saying we have changed for the better. Yet the thought will not down that a good thing can be pushed too far: the problem of being "pals" with our children is one of the hardest problems in existence.

We could simplify our task. We could begin this book, which shows fathers and children from various parts of the world, with gay or even pathetic stories. But we have more consideration for our readers, who intend to do more than just skim through the pictures.

Adam, the first man, came into this freshly created world as an adult. He was no child of woman born, but the son of the Heavenly Father, who created him in His own image. Nor did Eve have a mother. She was created from Adam's rib; and if those two children of God had not been so disobedient, who knows how everything would have turned out? At any rate, from the very outset it was the father who had to worry about his creatures. It was not until our forebears founded a family that the mother began to bear her share of the joys and sorrows involved for thousands of years now with the rearing of children.

Curiously enough, the mystery of mother and child has become far more universally accepted than that of father and child. The man of the house goes out into a hostile world and plays a part that sharply contrasts with that of the mother of his children. She remains at home, sagely running the household, teaching her daughters and protecting her sons. "How are things at home? How's your wife and kids?" Father hears that time and time again. Wife and kids, they go together.

The mother threatens the children: "Wait till your father gets home!" Often enough, indeed, she herself is afraid of him. Of the violent quarrels between father and son we shall not speak, even though they deserve some mention here. But something else occurs to us as we review the history of the father. He has always been in danger of becoming slightly ridiculous. His attempts to inflate his authority until he becomes tyrant of the house, before whom the rest of the family trembles, backfires and is met by jeers at his powerlessness. The angriest splutterer turns out to be helpless and finally does just what the mother (and the children) wanted him to do.

Even in the image of God the Heavenly Father and His creation, a little humor sneaks in. Zeus was a victim of Prometheus' laughter; and every one of us knows a whole string of jokes in which the father cuts a comic figure. We might mention Wilhelm Busch's "It's not hard to become a father," and "I am thy father Anchises and tell you only this!"—just to mention two examples. Even the father in the *Erlkönig* (king of the elves), the deeply devoted protector of his child, has become the butt of vulgar parodies.

Look in vain for as many jokes about the mother. That also must have its deep reasons. Perhaps it is the powerful father taboo of the West that arouses humor—as a method of defence. Let the reader come to his own conclusions.

One hoary myth of the "good old days," however, we must stoutly brand a lie. We boldly assert that it is more fun being a father today than at any time since the days of the patriarchs. Two generations ago a far-sighted woman predicted that the twentieth century would be the child's century. Despite two world wars, many upheavals, and even the advent of the atomic age, this prophecy has at least been partially fulfilled. A new age seems to have dawned for fathers—to the advantage of parents as well as children.

Some might scornfully point to the wretched plight of children throughout the world, especially among the much discussed underdeveloped peoples. We reply that our age has only now learned how to *see* this plight. But—to return to this book—since when have we had pictures of fathers and children as they really are? From the early days of Christianity, the theme of mother and child has been an inexhaustible source of inspiration for art, but only rarely do we see the earthly father Joseph even modestly occupying a corner of these pictures. Then there were church pictures, painted or carved in stone, depicting the whole family hierarchy of father, mother, sons and daughters, standing next to each other like organ pipes. They were not portrayed without love, to be sure, but much more as proud exhibits. The rococo loved the well-fed, allegorical, Cupid-like *putti*; the Biedermeier period gave us the sentimental family portrait with well-bred, freshly scrubbed children. Later came the rather stiff group pictures, the inevitable baby stretched out on a bearskin, and the confirmation child. We can think of one really moving exception: the picture of Napoleon III, already a sick man, with his grown son Lulu on his knee. It is the best early evidence of a really moving, tragic relationship between father and son, far removed from the polished niceties or boring frivolities of nineteenth-century portraiture. Then, too, there were pictures of the poor orphaned child—but without human impact. They were like Murillo's beggar children: full of graceful charm for all their misery, and in the final analysis as false as the pseudo-shepherds and shepherdesses.

Rarely now do we see these conventional children types and their world as defined by the grown-ups. The chief reason is that we adults, especially fathers, are different. The sharper, incorruptible camera lens was not alone in bringing about the transformation. After all, photography has been with us for many decades now. It is that we ourselves wanted to see our children in a new light. At bottom, it was the dissolution of modern society, the origins of which are complex and go considerably back in time, that loosened the ties between father and child. What we are harvesting today is the human fruit of our inhuman age.

8

We are omitting from this book virtually all the deeply stirring pictures of children from the more remote parts of the earth. We realize full well that fathers' hearts beat just as strongly for African and Chinese children. But here we are limiting ourselves in the main to our Western world, in fact, to the swiftly changing middle–class society with which we are most familiar. At the same time we openly acknowledge that, as far as children are concerned, whether here or in other parts of the world, we have not indulged in a kind of "literary" pity.

The ways of the human heart cannot be shortened by any technical progress. Whoever lacks eyes to see, is not aware of the more mysterious world. He cannot see either fathers or children in the bright and dark strands of their interwoven lives—on the street just below our window or in the far reaches of Africa and India. And even the person who is spiritually prepared to look with deep humanity into things often needs help from the writer and artist, and, increasingly in our time, from the photographer and movie-maker. This "opening the eyes" is one of the most important purposes of picture books like this one.

We realize that neither text nor pictures can capture all the relations between fathers and their children. Nor will it surprise us if some readers, expecting quite different experiences and opinions, see things in a much gayer or graver light. But as we usher the reader into this world of pictures, even the brightest of which is rooted in the dark soil of our troubled time, we do so with advice from a half–forgotten German poet, Leopold Schefer: "Spend lots of time with your children! Have them near you day and night and love them. And let yourself be loved in those wonderful years that never will return!"

CREDITS

Front cover picture: Germany
   Elisabeth Niggemeyer
Back cover picture: Germany
   I. Donderer—*Ullstein*
1. USA Nolan Patterson—
Collignon
2. England Kosmos—*Collignon*
3. France Paul Almasy
4. Germany Elisabeth Niggemeyer
5. USA Carroll Seghers—
Collignon
6. England, training course for
mothers Kosmos—*Col-
lignon*
7. South Africa Irmin Henkel
8. Germany Hans Speck—
Bayerische Bild GmbH.
9. Canada Eric Scott
10. China Hilmar Pabel
11. Austria Inge Loeffler
12. Italy Anita Niesz
13. Polo Rivel with his children
I. Donderer—*Ullstein*
14. USA Harvey Shaman
15. Germany Renate Bein—
alpha
16. Sweden Sven Joseph
17. Germany Mathilde Runte
18. USSR Georg Oddner
19. Germany Hans A. Comotio
20. Austria Seiler—*Anthony*
21. France Henri Cartier-
Bresson—*Magnum*
22. Otto von Habsburg with his
daughter Paul Almasy
23. Germany Elisabeth Niggemeyer
24. India Rudi Herzog
25. USA Kit Robbins—*Rapho*
26. Mexico Armin Haab
27. Spain Fulvio Roiter
28. Headhunters from Luzon,
the Philippines John Everard
29. Cambodia R. Cauchetier
30. Tunisia René Burri—*Magnum*
31. Afghanistan Franz Perabo
32. India Jean-Phan-Chan The
33. Ecuador Fed. Patellani
34. Germany Fritz Fenzl

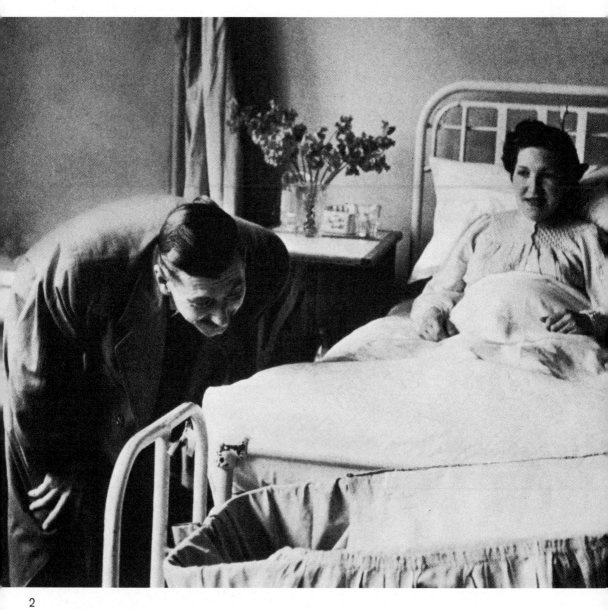

3

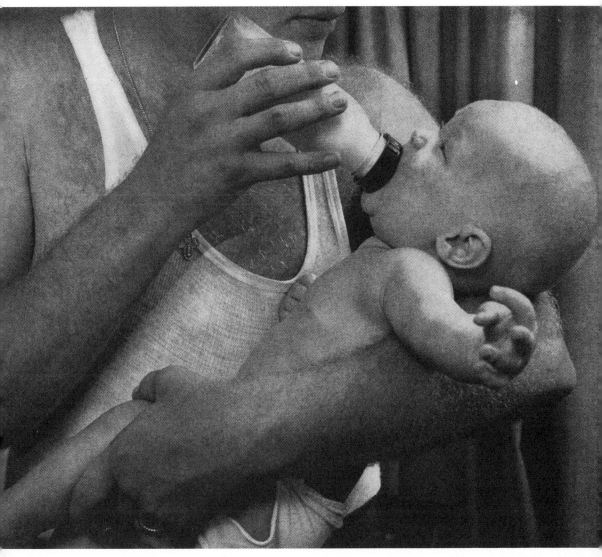

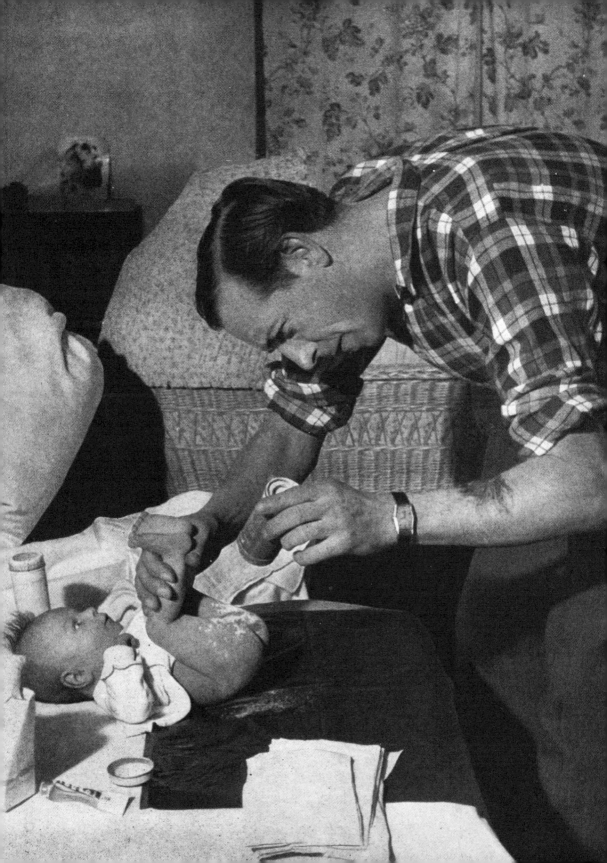

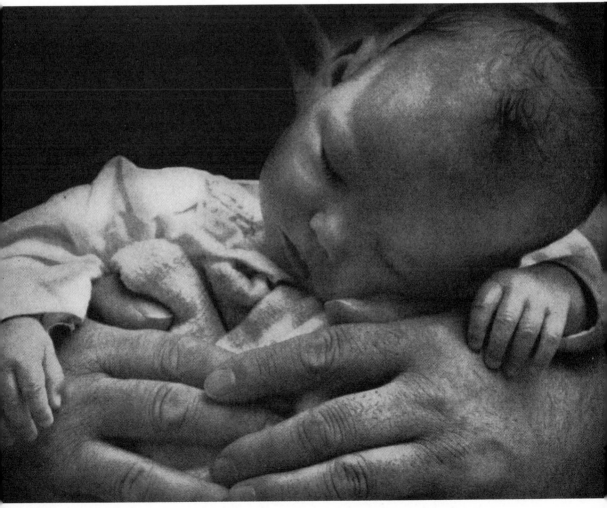

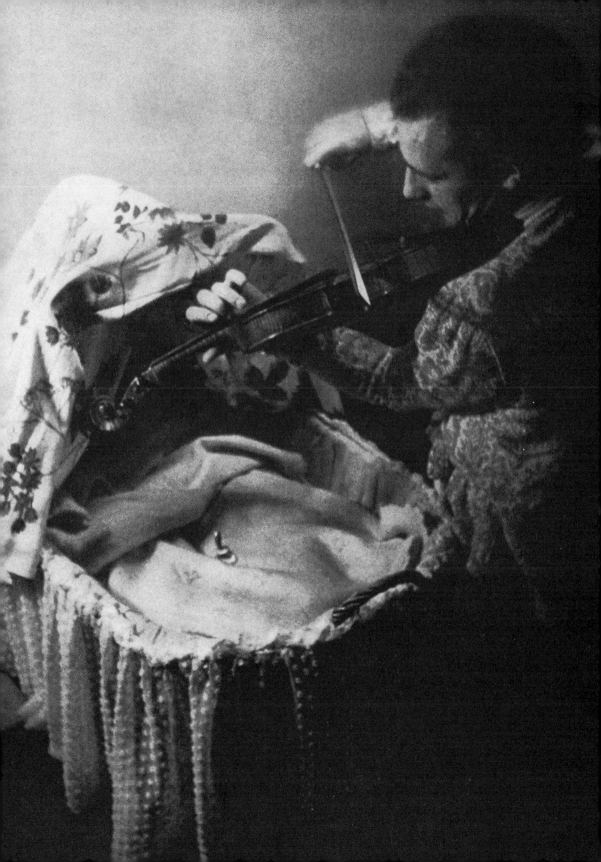

14

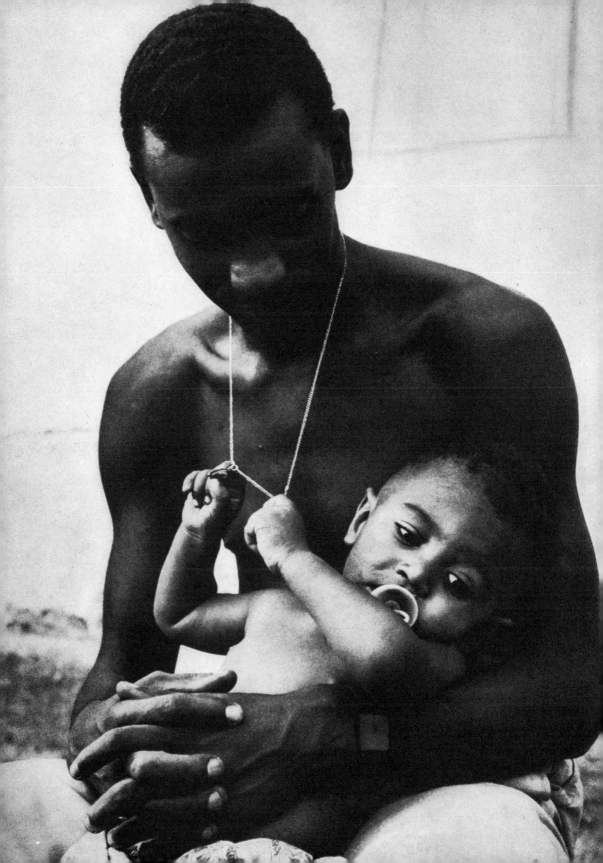

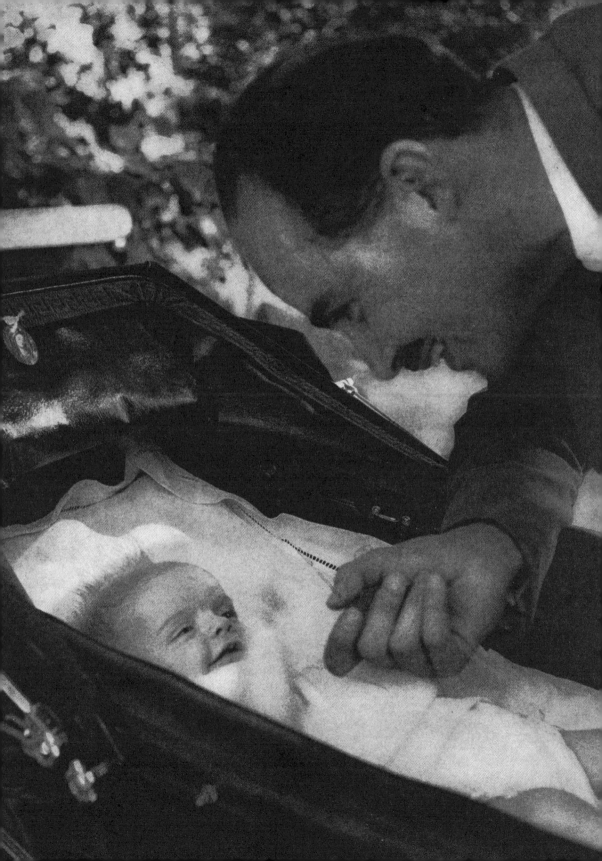

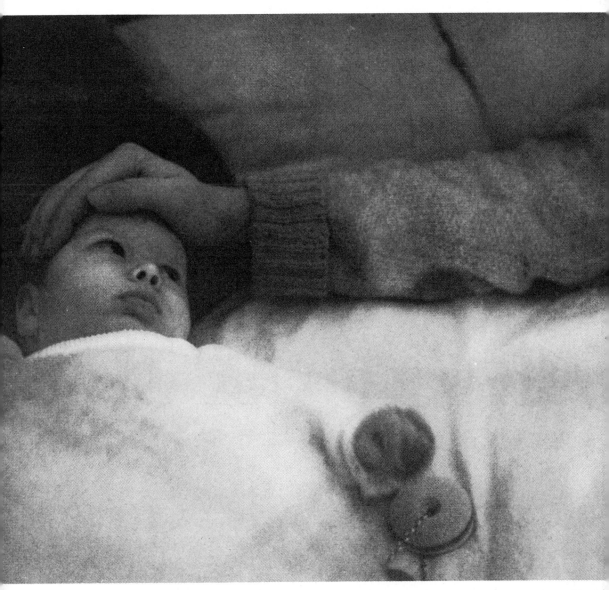

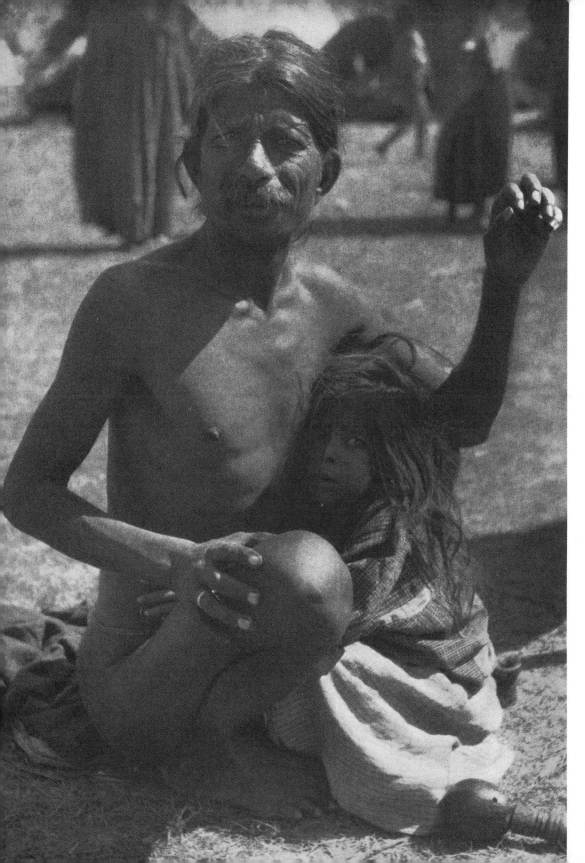

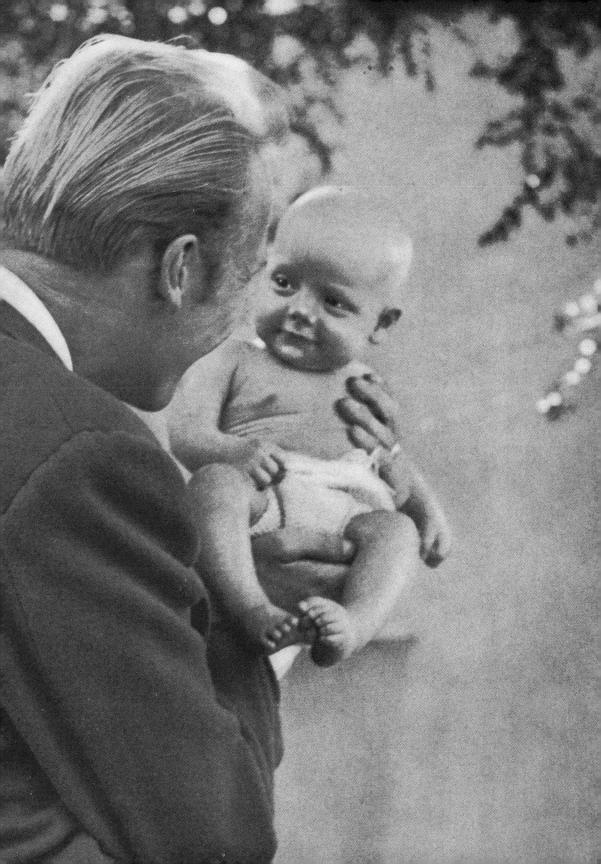

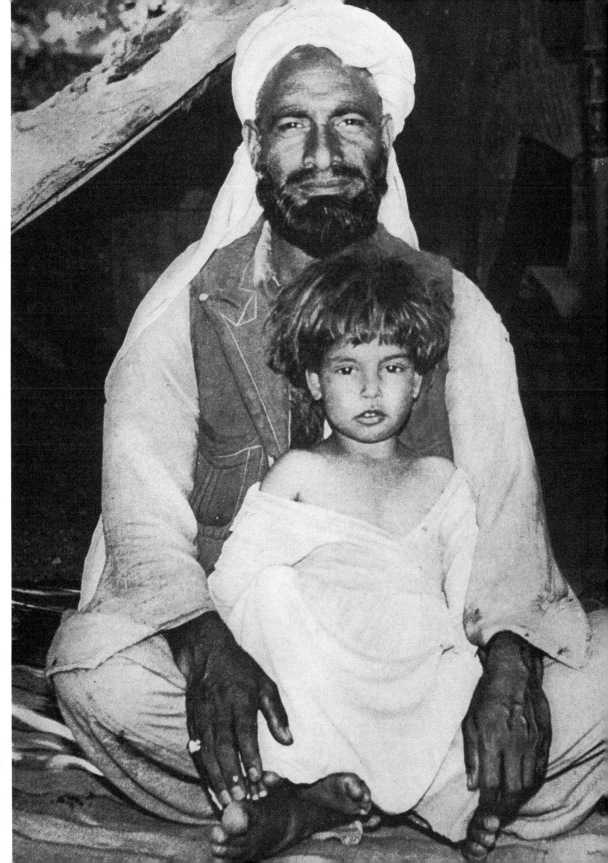

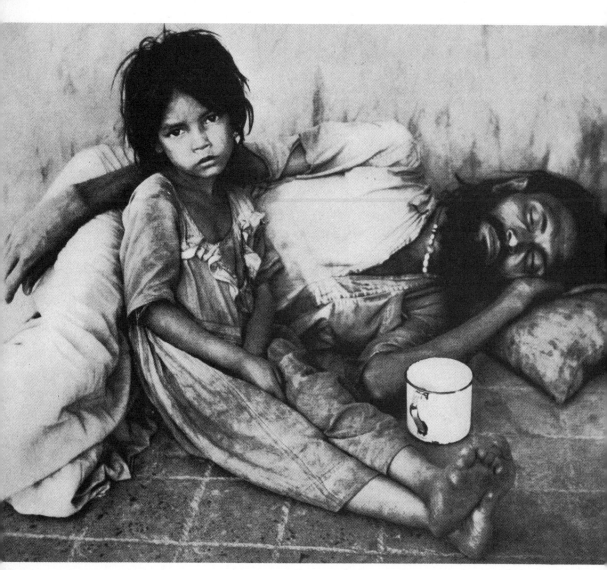

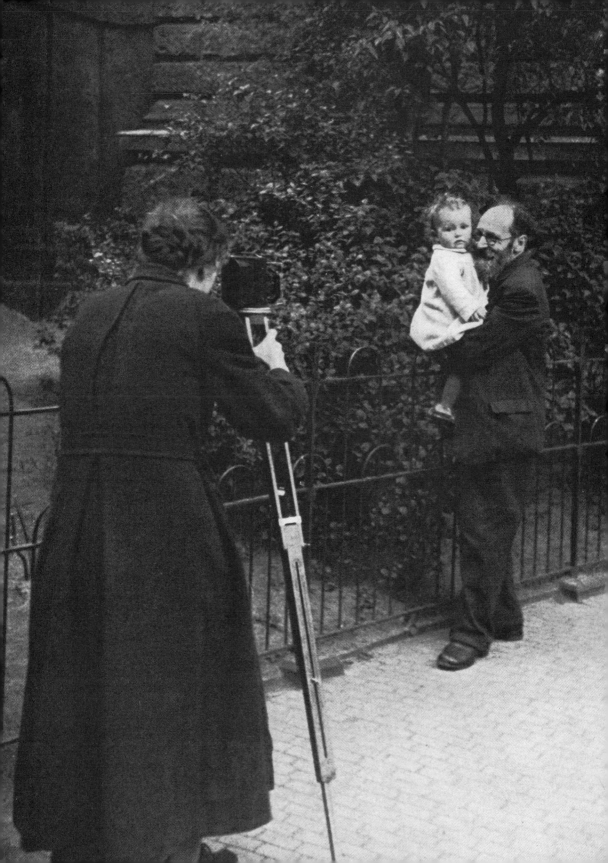